Where Will I Make My Nest?

First edition
ISBN 978-1-8380280-3-9

Where Will I Make My Nest?

www.davidhutchison.co.uk

Where Will I Make My Nest?

Book 1 in the Seordag Stories series

David Hutchison

A rubbish tip is on fire. Soley, a seagull with a wooden leg, is circling. He spies a plastic carton and soars down to investigate.

"Mmmh, smells like Vindaloo, my favourite. Oh my," says Soley as he pecks at the curry. Suddenly the carton lurches.

Soley squawks and flies up onto an old vacuum cleaner. Seordag, a robot hen with a TV stomach, rises up out of the rubbish, her tail smouldering. Seordag gasps,"Phew, hot, hot!"

Seordag dumps her tail into a pan of water.
"Oooohhhh, that's better!"
Soley hops down and looks for the curry.

Soley asks, "Who are you?"
The robot hen replies, "I'm Seordag."
Soley says, "I'm Soley. It's no use, I'll never find the curry now."

Soley hasn't noticed the fire getting closer.
Soley says, "Mmmmh, that smells good. What is it?"

Seordag replies,"You!"
Soley soars squawking up into the air.

Soley cools off in a puddle. Seordag clambers over the pile of junk heading for a gate.

Soley says, "Where are you going?"
Seordag replies, " I'm off to find a good place to make my nest."
Soley says, "Blarag has a nice big barn."

Seordag says,"Who's Blarag?"
Soley replies,"Oh, he's a friend of mine. It's not far. Come on."

Off they go along a path.

As they come around a corner they hear fiddle music and see a barn with a rusty iron roof and large wooden doors.

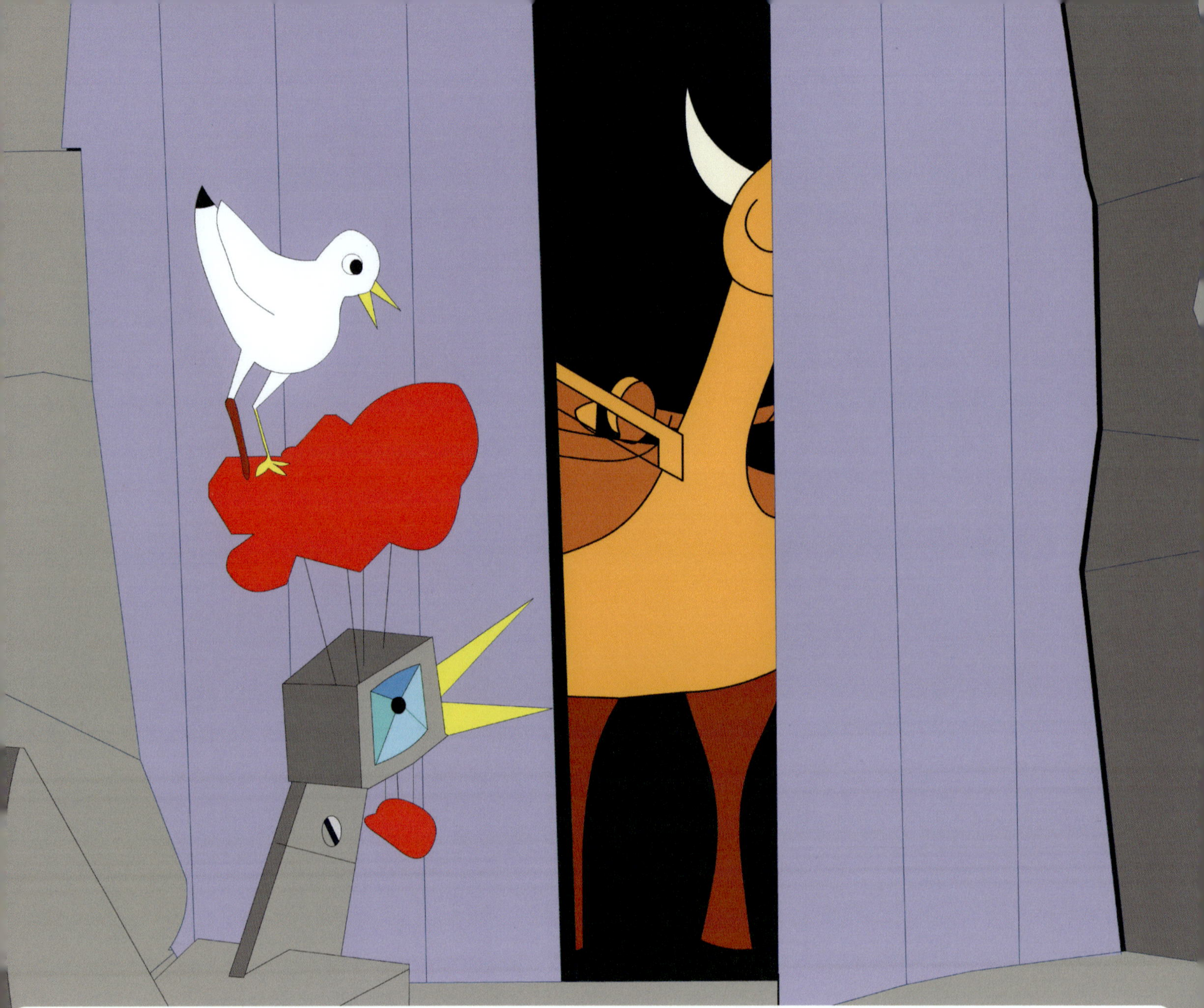

Seordag taps on the door. The fiddling stops. Blarag opens the door. Soley says,"Seordag is looking for a nice place to make a nest. Have you any room?"

Blarag says, "I've got plenty of space. Have a look around."
The floor is covered with music sheets.
Seordag says, "What a grand place you have here!"

Seordag thinks. Her TV shows her nest already built and containing three eggs. Some music sheets blow in a breeze, hiding the eggs. Blarag stands on the eggs by accident.

Seordag says, "Thanks, but I don't think it's a good place to build my nest." Soley and Blarag nod in agreement.

"Maybe Ewella can help?" says Blarag.
"Yes, she has plenty of space," replies Soley, "let's go and see her!"
Seordag,Blarag and Soley set off along the winding path.

Crossing a bridge they head for a sheep pen with a dipping pool.
A strange sound comes from the pool.
Soley squawks, "Sounds like she's having a dip."

Ewella crawls out of the pool and says, "Hi. Who is your friend?"
Blarag replies," This is Seordag. She's looking for a place to make a nest."
Ewella says,"I've got plenty of room. Have a look around."

Seordag thinks on her TV. Rain comes down and the nest slithers into the dipping pool.
Seordag sighs,"I don't think there is enough shelter here."

Soley says, "I saw a metal kind of nest, where Marlene the Crofter was working."
Blarag, "Let's have a look!"

So they set off along the path again and come across a cement mixer in a small clearing. Nearby, Marlene the Crofter is mending a fence.

Soley squawks, "This is it."
Seordag has a look around.

Seordag looks in the cement mixer. She thinks on her TV.

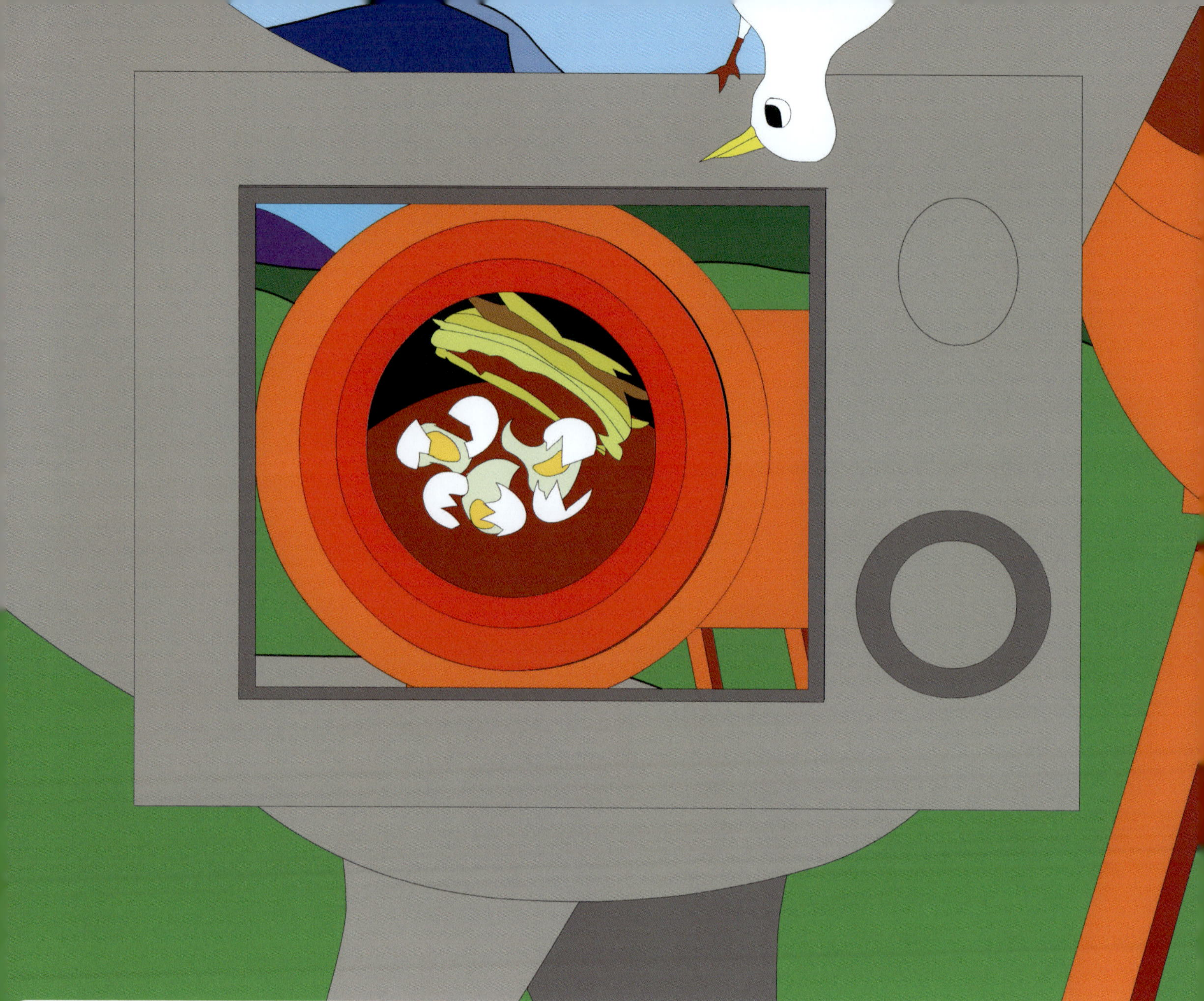

The nest is in the cement mixer.
The mixer starts to spin ...
...and all the eggs are smashed.

Seordag says, "Will I ever find a place to make my nest?"
Seordag and the others start walking along the path again.

The cement mixer says in a growling voice, "Marlene , you know how your TV's broken? A TV hen called Seordag just went past. She's looking for somewhere to build a nest."

Marlene shouts, "Seordag!"
Seordag and the others come back.

Marlene says,"You need a nest and my TV's broken. If we all help, we could make you a fabulous hen house and tonight we could all watch my favourite programme on your belly!"

Seordag asks, "Where will we build it?"
Marlene replies, "There, on top of the old ruin."

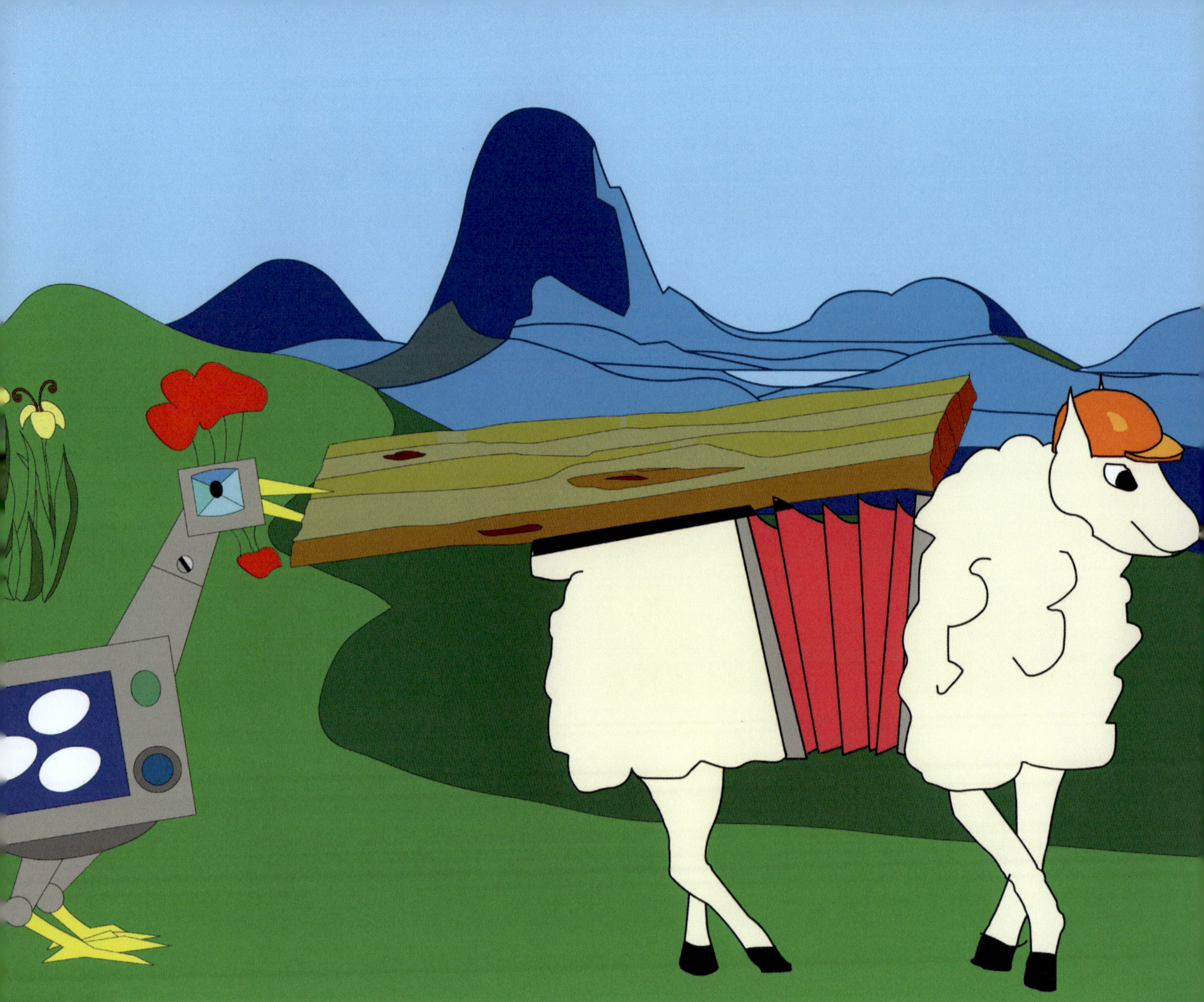

Ewella and Seordag carry planks of wood between them.

Cement Mixer churns out concrete. Seordag uses a trowel in her beak to spread the concrete as Marlene builds the foundations. Ewella brings everyone tea.

At last the hen house is finished.
Seordag says, "This is wonderful."

Seordag sits in the hen house, makes a nest and lays her eggs. She gets off the nest to show the others the three new shiny eggs.

The eggs hatch and three mobile phone chicks emerge, making chirpy ringtones.

Marlene and Ewella dance together. Blarag plays his fiddle.
Seordag laughs,"I'm so happy, I have great friends, three lovely chicks, a beautiful hen house and a ceilidh to end the day!"

Printed in Poland
by Amazon Fulfillment
Poland Sp. z o.o., Wrocław

62655331R00026